THE CHINA BLACKBIRD

MIKE PEARCE

Copyright 2018 by Mike Pearce

All rights reserved. No part of this book may be reproduced, distributed or transmitted in any form or by any means, including photocopying, recording, or other electronic or mechanical methods, without the prior written permission of the author, except in the case of brief quotations embodied in reviews and certain other non-commercial uses permitted by copyright law. You must not circulate this book in any format.

This book may not be resold or given away to other people. Please respect the work of the author and purchase a copy for you own use.

This is a fictional work and all characters are drawn from the author's imagination. Any resemblance or similarities to persons living or dead are entirely coincidental

ISBN:10-1987474112
ISBN-13:978-1987474114

DEDICATION

This book is dedicated to all bird lovers and those who
feed birds

CONTENTS

ACKNOWLEDGMENTS

The author would like to thank Christine Pearce
for reading and checking through the manuscript.

PREFACE

This fictional story was written in winter. Not like a normal winter. Rain, when it landed quickly, froze and ice completely covered the roads and anything in sight. This affected every living creature, some more than others including birds and in this case a blackbird.

1 THE BLACKBIRD

High up on a top shelf on a dresser in Nellie's back room stood a china blackbird. It had been bought one Saturday morning in a small market. There was a choice of birds, robins, blue tits, and blackbirds. Nellie had chosen a blackbird as she had a pair of blackbirds in her garden. As with her other ornaments it was put on the top of a large dresser as there was no more room on her mantlepiece. It was a good dust catcher.

The last time Nellie had taken it down it fell off and broke its bright orange beak. This was glued back on and no one could see the join. There the blackbird stayed undisturbed for several years. Nellie never married and was quite content living on her own. She always said when someone asked her why she didn't marry that she preferred to read a book or eat a cream scone. She loved birds, all birds, and one would often see her down by the village pond feeding the ducks. She even wore a hat that had a crested top raised high with ostrich feathers.

A male blackbird lived at the bottom of the garden. Its feathers were glossy and as black as coal. Its beak was bright yellowy orange and its legs blackish brown. It had yellow eye rings. Its partner was not black but very dark brown with a whitish throat. It loved to hop along the fence and sit on the highest tree singing a whole melodious medley of different trills and songs, especially from March to June. It would run after other birds raising its tail when it landed to show that Nellie's garden was part of its territory. It was the first bird to come out in the morning at first light when it would sing. It also sang as the sun was setting and if near any street lamps.

2 SNOW

The snow had arrived and everyone said how nice it looked. Schools were closed. People struggled to get to work. The snow was from the Arctic. It was the only time we got snow; the roads were clear, but the side roads and gardens remained covered. The sun came out that afternoon and the birds became more active. That night the temperature dropped to -4 degrees centigrade and any water outside froze solid within minutes. Peoples' outlets from sinks froze up. The temperature then went up to zero and the bitter wind dropped. Morning came, and the wind was back as bitter as ever creeping into every crevice as it blew hurtling from the sea. It was 6 o'clock and it tried to snow but couldn't. It rained, covering everything in sight, leaving a thick coating of ice like icing sugar. Walls, cars, roads, everything was covered in a layer of ice. There was no sun and the temperature remained at -3 degrees centigrade with no prospect of changing.

The birds had seen snow before. It was a yearly norm.

Even in the snow the blackbirds would look bright and healthy. They were always searching for food to eat amongst the fallen leaves so as to keep warm. They wrapped up warm in their extra covering of feathers which they would fluff up their feathers for insulation trapping more air. They also had more fat on them than in the summer. Extra food was provided by many home owners at this time. They roosted at night in sheltered areas and in trees which still had their leaves. It was too cold to sing on this day when the rain froze and even too cold to expend too much energy.

Flying down to the garden to eat food.it had started to snow again. This time the snow was not small roundish heavy flakes but fine flat flakes which with the strong wind stuck onto the sides and branches of trees and fences. A black bird flew down onto the fence followed by its wife who was browner in colour. They had been in this garden which was part of their territory for 10 years and had seen the seasons come and go.

In this garden were apple and pear trees and much of

the fruit that fell was left on the ground. Spiders, invertebrates and berries also formed the bird's diet and as it was a chalky garden it was not difficult to find snails hiding under plastic flower pots on the ground. The blackbirds were not the only pair visiting the garden. Their sons and daughters also often came to visit. They were always very careful birds with a keen eye and would produce a warning song if anything dangerous came in view. The black birds could deal with snow which covered branches and fences which could make flying and landing difficult.

3 ICED

Birds can still die in very freezing weather. They try to avoid wind-chill and sit in thick evergreen vegetation often on the lower branches, so they can hop down and look for food in the day. Some can go into torpor at night, their heart rate and metabolism slowing down

The blackbird which ventured out from the tree was hit by a sudden fall in temperature as the rain fell. The wind was constantly changing direction, so the bird had to move round to try and face the wind so as to prevent it lifting up its feathers from behind and making it colder. It was on the ground and raised its wings to fly back to the tree. It tried to flap but the wind was so cold, and the rain had frozen, even clinging onto the surface of the wing feathers which became stuck together with ice.

It tried again but to no avail. It put its bill under its shoulder feathers so that it could breathe in the warm air under there. It decided to hop across the lawn and shelter under a bush to get out of the wind and rain.

Here it could try and peck the ice off its wings and have another attempt at making it back to the fir tree. Its feet didn't feel the cold as the circulation was redirected away from the legs. It tried to lift one of its matchstick like legs from off the grass, but it found was stuck to the ground in a sheet of ice. It tried the other leg, but it too was also frozen to the ground. The constant downpour of rain made the layer of ice over its feet even thicker, pinning it to that spot on the lawn like a statue. All around him it could hear the pitiful cries from other birds sitting on twigs as they too became frozen with the ice. All the twigs glistened, being covered with a layer of ice. Even leaves were coated in ice and the cells inside were frozen and burst never again to recover when the ice at last thawed.

Flowering plants in the garden were also affected in the same way. It was supposed to be the start of spring. The blackbird heard a noise in a nearby bush and saw that some of the sparrows that had been sitting there were falling to the ground like hailstones, frozen solid. There must have been several dozen.

Those remaining were frozen by their feet to the twigs. The blackbird was very scared and struggled, but by struggling exerted more energy and it became colder. It gave a faint chirp to call his wife, but she could not hear it. Its little eyes slowly closed and froze over. The rain continued to fall covering the bird with frozen ice. It had fed well a few days before in order to survive a cold spell but not one as cold as this.

Sadly there it stood, frozen solid, covered in ice, like a lonely varnish covered ornament in a shop window. In the daylight it looked as if it had been preserved in glass. No other birds or small animals were out at this time. If there were foxes or cats they would have quickly made a meal of them, but every animal was sheltering.

Nellie wanted to go outside to put something in the bin. She was also concerned that she had not turned off the water to the outside tap. She undid the bolt and opened the back door and saw it was very icy. She went back indoors and put on a thick coat, gloves and a woolly hat and went to the cupboard to take out a container of table salt. She opened the back door and sprinkled the salt onto the back step and onto the path next to the bin which was near the grass. The bin was covered in ice, so she picked up a stone from the ground and gave it a bash so that the ice fell off. This instant freeze of the fallen rain that had fallen, covered walls, windows and the ground. She opened up the bin and threw the rubbish inside and dropped the lid back down. More ice fell off the sides. The rain landing on her coat was freezing as it fell giving it a shine. She looked across the garden and could see a small black object. She carefully walked over and saw there was a blackbird frozen to the ground. She thought she could pick it up, but lifting it might pull its legs off, so she stamped on the ice around it with her foot which broke and lifted the bird up with its little ice platform. She held it carefully as she knew if she hit it, it may damage the poor bird.

4 ATTEMPTS AT REVIVAL

She brought the blackbird inside and stood it on a tray in the middle of the table. Her house was warm, a lot warmer than outside. She pondered what to do. Should she put it next to the steam from her kettle or let it just thaw. She decided to go upstairs and bring down her hairdryer. That would melt the ice slowly and all over the bird. When she came down she switched the hairdryer on but did not want to melt the ice first around the feet as it would topple over. She decided to lay it down on its side, so it wouldn't fall. She concentrated the warm air mainly on its face and chest so that the warm air would help it breathe again. She had read that sometimes young children had fallen into icy water they had survived as their metabolism had slowed down as had their heart rate. But for the black bird this seemed not to be the case. It just lay there lifeless completely still. She lifted its head up and its wings, but they just flopped back down again onto the tray. She felt very sad. She'd seen this little bird in her garden for many years and thrown out bread and apples on the lawn for it. No longer would she hear the lovely selection of songs it sang as the sun began to set.

She left the bird on the table and she slumped down in her arm chair and pulled a blanket over her. She would be glad when all this freezing weather was over and she could sit outside in the sunshine. She turned on the radio and heard that the driving was treacherous. People were advised to stay indoors as the roads were covered in black ice caused by the freezing rain. She also heard that on the beaches thousands of starfish had been washed up where they had been dislodged by the rough seas and had frozen to death. Hundreds of seagulls were feeding on them.

5 BROKEN BUT LIVING

She fell asleep. It was warm under the blanket and the radio was playing soft music. Crash! "What was that?" She woke up with a sudden start. She stood up and looked around. On the floor beneath the dresser lay her blackbird not the one she had brought in from the garden, but the china one that had sat up on the dresser. There it was now in pieces, its beak once again broken off but now its body was in several pieces. She bent down to pick them up when all of a sudden, she heard a song, a bird song.

She looked up and saw a blackbird up on the dresser where her china bird had stood. She put on her glasses and saw it was alive, she was overjoyed. It was the bird she had placed on the tray. She let it fly all around the room and fed it some bread, some corn and cornflakes. She would not let it out again that day as it might freeze again.

The next day she got up early and went downstairs. The temperature was now four degrees centigrade.

There was no rain and the sun was out. Much of the ice had melted. The blackbird was fluttering against her window. It could see its partner hopping about on the grass. She opened the window and out it flew straight away to join its partner. It spent the day establishing its territory which it did at this time of the year. Once established the pair would build a nest at the bottom of her garden in the ivy as they always did. Nellie was happy once again. In the summer she would continue to sit out on her veranda and enjoy the summer evenings waiting for the song of her blackbird at sunset. She was even awoken very early in the morning at sunrise when the bird sang outside her window.

Morning has broken like the first morning

Blackbird has spoken like the first bird

Praise for the singing

Praise for the morning

Praise for them springing fresh from the world

Eleanor Farjeon (1931)

To see other publications below by the author visit
snappysnappybooks.com

<u>The really, really, really useful series</u>

How to be a Successful Business Weed
How to Deal with Life's Snakes and Ladders
Know Your Students and Build Your Image
Pens for Pops
How to be a Successful Charity Shop
Make up-revealed
Ronnie's Sermon snippets
Wastefulness-Bone and Urine
Fertility Stones and Chocolate Eggs
Clingers, creepers and scramblers
I Herring Gull
Viking Bay-Natural History

<u>Other books by Mike Pearce:</u>

Pattern for Purpose- God's and Man's designs
Red Fred Cell and Friends
Human Termites eat London
Pigeons Splat London
Glass Anemones Tentacle-ize London
Tuppeny Hangover
I am Termite
The littlest Oyster
Bits and Bobs
The Shell Man
Cats at Christmas
Tails, Tales
Trust-Nothing but a Must
In a Dark, Dark Corner was the Holy Ghost
The Shell Lady
Captain Grottbuster versus the Grey World

London's Nemesis (Trilogy of 3, 4 and 5 above
Saved by Angels (Trilogy of 6, 8 and 14 above)
The World of Wax
Photosynthetic Women
Queen Rat on Deadman's Island
The Watcher on the Fal
The Rock Pool
The Little Shepherd Boy's Gift
The Living Fossils
Old Mother Nature Laughed and Laughed
Betty's Barcodes
Time Runs Dry (play)
Valentines Cards
The Scrofula Infirmary
The Cornish Urchin
My Therizinosaurus
Spider in the Tomb
The White Cockerel
The Red Church Doll
Butterfly Angels (compilation of previous books)
The Girl Under the Paeony Tree
Baby Feet
The Sparrows' Last Soul
Ball Rooms
Absorbed by a Woman
St Mildred-Patron Saint of Thanet
The Slothful Wife
The Tuppeny Bear
The Boy who found Christmas
Nothing but leaves
The Giant's Toothpick
The Night Mare
The Old Pot and the Golden Shoes
Sitting next to Angels

Exodus to a leaf
The forlorn fruit fly
The Pawnbroker's Souls
The Nursery Rhyme Cat
A Call Under the Sea
Dead Donkey Lane
A Googolplex of Mice
The Eggstraordinary Easter Egg

ABOUT THE AUTHOR

Dr Mike Pearce is a scientist interested in behaviour. He also was a lecturer in human biology and health at a college in Canterbury, Kent